ELI, INCLUDED

"Inclusion isn't charity for one person,
it's a gift to everyone."

- Michelle Sullivan

This book is dedicated to Eli, my son.
You have opened my eyes to a magical
world I never saw before. You have opened
my heart and shown me how to love and
include people that are different. I will never
be the same and for that I am so grateful.

HEY!

KEEP AN EYE OUT FOR NUMBERS!

(HINT: ALL THE NUMBERS IN THIS BOOK HAVE A SPECIAL MEANING)

The students in room 46 are getting a new student today.

His name is Eli.

Eli wonders why the hooks are so high.

During craft time, his self portrait doesn't quite look like everyone else's.

Eli asks what the classroom pets names are.

Miss Hillary says, "Okay class, we have a new student. His name is Eli. Eli, will you come introduce yourself?"

Eli says that he has 3 sisters and his favorite things are ice cream and lions.

"Great question,"
says Miss Hillary.

"You've got braces
on your teeth to move
them into the right spot,
well that's the same reason Eli has
braces on his feet. His muscles aren't
quite as strong as yours, so the braces
help his feet stay in the right place so
he can walk, run and jump just like you."

"Eli has something called Down syndrome."

Miss Hillary says, "No, you can't catch Down syndrome. We all have chromosomes in our body. Chromosomes are our bodies instructions on what makes you uniquely you."

"Down syndrome is when your body has 3 copies of the 21st chromosome."

"Chromosomes are what make me have curly hair, green eyes and freckles."

Under her breath Miss Hillary says something about her ex-fiancé having cold feet, but the children don't quite understand what that means.

"Eli's 47 chromosomes decided that he would have blonde curly hair, and that he would be a little shorter than most people."

glasses

"There are lots of things that have helped Eli move and grow.

Glasses to see far,

gait trainer

a gait trainer to help him learn to walk,

braces

braces (or orthotics) to keep his feet straight,

and a feeding tube that puts food right into his stomach."

feeding tube

Billy, who hates the taste of broccoli, thought that sounded pretty cool.

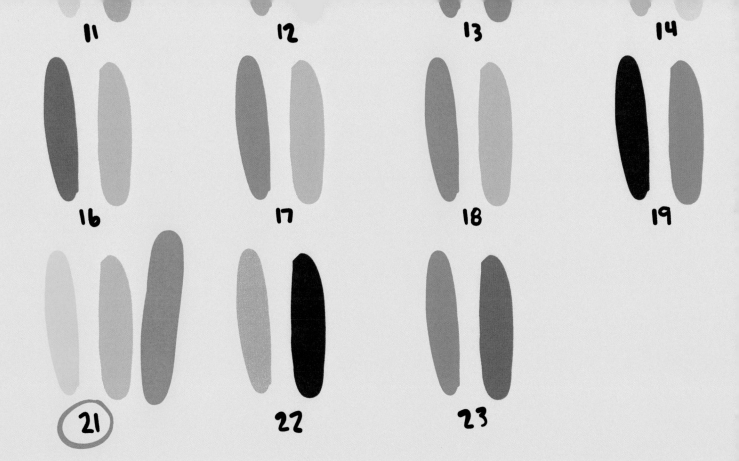

11   12   13   14

16   17   18   19

(21)   22   23

Miss Hillary says, "We are all different, how boring would it be if we were all the same? But it's great that we can all enjoy things together."

Eli said he likes ice cream and lions and he has sisters. What about you?

The bell rings for lunch. Eli is a little nervous about where to sit.

Both Eli and Billy are so glad to have made a new friend.

QUESTIONS YOU MAY HAVE ABOUT DOWN SYNDROME:

Q: *Can you catch it?*

A: **Nope! People are born with Down syndrome just like you were born with the color eyes you have. It's not contagious.**

Q: *How are people with Down syndrome different?*

A: **Some kids with Down syndrome may need extra help in school. They may have an aide that helps them with their schoolwork. They may go to extra classes called therapy to help them with things like using scissors and writing.**

Q: *What can I do?*

A: **You can treat people with Down syndrome just like everyone else. Everyone needs friends and everyone likes to play, so go have fun together. You can start by asking them what their favorite flavor of ice cream is. ☺**

DID YOU FIND ALL OF THE SPECIAL NUMBERS?

Most people have 46 chromosomes

When someone has 3 copies of the 21st chromosome, they have Down syndrome

Most people have 2 copies of the 21st chromosome, but people that have 3 copies have Down syndrome

Goldfish have 94 chromosomes

People with Down syndrome have 47 chromosomes

Guinea pigs have 64 chromosomes

Chameleons have 24 chromosomes

ABOUT THE AUTHOR

Michelle Sullivan owns *Littlest Warrior Apparel* and is the host of *Advocate Like a Mother* podcast. Michelle lives in Orange County, CA and is married to her high school sweetheart, Eric. They have 3 teenage girls and their 5 year old son Eli, who has Down syndrome and a heart defect. Eli opened Michelle's eyes to the world of advocacy.

Michelle is passionate about showing people their worth – whether it's someone with special needs, or a woman who has yet to see herself through God's eyes.

You can follow Michelle on Instagram:

@meeshellsullivan
@littlest_warrior
@advocatelikeamother

ABOUT THE ILLUSTRATOR

Britt Scott is an illustrator and children's writer. To see more of her work or to contact her, visit her website: brittscottillustration.com, or follow her on instagram: @britt_adrift.

IF YOU LOVE THIS BOOK, PLEASE SHARE AND USE #ELIINCLUDED

10307397R00024

Made in the USA
Monee, IL
26 August 2019